Psychic Development
by
Margaret West

Psychic Development

ISBN: 978-1-907963-09-4

Published by

Hedge Witchery Books

www.hedge-witcherybooks.com

Copyright © Margaret West 2012

All rights reserved No part of this publication may be reproduced, stored in a retrieval system, or transmitted by any forms or by any means, electronic, mechanical, photocopying, recording or otherwise, without the prior permission of the copyright owner.

Brief quotations may be used for review and promotional purposes without gaining prior permission if less than 300 words are used.

Introduction

Margaret West has been a Light worker for over 30 years. A Clairknowing medium, Usui Reiki Master/Teacher, Angelic Reiki Master/Teacher, Angel Therapist, Crystal Therapist and teacher of many metaphysical studies, she also is an author of many paranormal/romance and non-fiction books.

Her latest non-fiction book on Psychic Development explains the journey to enlightenment in an easy and understandable term. Each lesson is designed by Margaret, to open up the psychic centres inherent in all of us.

It is no coincidence that you have been drawn to read this book. Nothing happens by chance. Threads are never left dangling in the spirit world. You are being lead to a subject from those in spirit who wish to nurture your spiritual growth. Pay attention to their gentle prodding.

Margaret's Spiritual website can be found here: www.connectionswithspirit.co.uk

Margaret's writer's website can be found here: www.margaretwest.net

Acknowledgements

My greatest thanks to:

Cheryl Turtlemoon: For the cover art to this book which was channelled through her by the angels and for supplying the aura pictures. www.cherylsangels.co.uk

Joe Prentice: For some of the wonderful scenic pictures he has taken and supplied for this book.

Jake the photographer: Whose scenic pictures in this book are truly magnificent.

Betty Masters: President of Sutton Spiritualist church, great friend and spiritual teacher who taught me so much about the spirit side of life.

Julie Hayes: A fabulous author, editor and friend. Who always finds time to help me with every aspect of my writing. http://julielynnhayes.blogspot.com

Carole Owens: A friend and fellow blogger who took and donated the beautiful Bluebell picture for this book. http://smockturtle.blogspot.com

Skyla Wilde: For allowing me to use the picture of her as angel, from her modelling portfolio.

Phil Mortiboy: For the beautiful picture of his guide.

George Edwards: For his wonderful psychic art drawing of a Native American spirit guide.

This book is dedicated to the spirit people who have guided, prodded and helped me on a wonderful spiritual journey of enlightenment that has spanned over 30 years.

My Master guide. Magenta and his helper Martha

My Spirit Guide: Anahey

My Crystal Therapy spiritual helper: Deserai

My spiritual writing helper: Sebastian

My teaching guides that are too many to mention, but whose guidance and wisdom has been invaluable.

My Guardian Angel: John

My Angel for this lifetime: Daniel.

To all the spiritual helpers that are past, present and yet to come, I humbly thank you.

Being Psychic

Some people, who are naturally connected to the spirit world, fear their ability. This tiny word 'Fear' is a powerful force to be reckoned with. It can grow astoundingly fast, just because we fail to understand ourselves. It's human nature to fear the unknown. People are scared they will 'see' something bad. So they ignore their abilities. Let me say here and now, nothing is bad. If a person views everything that they see as an opportunity to understand something new or help someone along their path in life, then what they 'see' will always be a good thing.

We need to acknowledge a harsh fact of life that at some point we will ALL die. It is a sad part of living. Unfortunately, some people will leave their earthly life earlier than others. There is no rhyme or reason, no cosmic order to it. We strive for years to make sense of it all, yet there is nothing really to understand. Death is just a fact of living in the now. We are all blue printed with an ability to understand life and death. It explains that death is not the end, but the beginning of a whole new different journey. But for some reason the translation gets lost in the powerful emotions we feel when we lose a loved one. This might be a part of the human existence that we have to go through. To learn from these emotions and react to them in a way that can help us to heal.

We are ALL psychic. There are no 'special gifted' people out there. Everyone has this protective mechanism that's designed to warn us about danger right from birth. But somehow this inherent ability became affiliated with the devil. People became terrified of it and our psychic senses became buried deep within us. The good news is that it can still be tapped into. The ability hasn't gone, it's just dormant.

When people first develop their psychic abilities, they need to learn how to discern between a true vision and a picture that their ego might be creating, and this can be very frightening. But let's break fear down and see it for what it truly is.

Fear is programmed into the nervous system at birth. It is our deepest survival instinct and it's there to protect us from danger. Many people try to hide the fact that they are scared, as they view it as a weakness, but in reality the emotion has an important function. It's our personal inbuilt warning device that tells us about the unknown and if something might be difficult or dangerous. Fear makes us sit up and pay attention to a situation we're in. Our brain reacts instantly to the emotion and will send signals to the nervous system to alert the body. The heartbeat will then quicken, the breath becomes faster and the blood pumps to muscle groups to prepare the body for physical action such as "fight or flight". The body stays in this state of flux until the brain receives a message saying the danger has passed.

This is why we must never eradicate fear from our lives. If we did manage to somehow do it, we would do dangerous even fatal things without thinking them through. But what we must never do is let fear rule our lives. We must always strive to bring it into proper balance and never allow it to stop us doing what we need to do to progress in life.

As this book is read, the lessons and exercises followed, your psychic centres will begin to naturally awaken. There's no need to rush to get to the next level of your Psychic Development. This journey of self-discovery is to be enjoyed. Learn from it and incorporate the knowledge attained into your everyday life.

Getting Started

Psychic Development isn't all about contacting the spirit world, but we do need to develop a connection, to enable us to develop psychically. This is nothing to be worried about. The people we contact in the spirit world, to help with our development, are highly evolved teachers who have chosen to help the living re-find themselves.

Everyone, when they first start connecting to the spirit world, will believe that what they are receiving are their own thoughts and not anything to do with their intuition or spirit guides/helpers. But it's natural to be suspicious, especially as we're dealing with a force that cannot be seen. As human beings it's ingrained within us to get concrete proof that what we see or feel is real. Sometimes we become impatient and want all the information in one go. I advocate not waiting for that to happen, because it never will. We live in a physical world, so it stands to reason that we think in physical terms. To believe in other forces, we must first start to believe in ourselves.

Anything that appears to be outside our normal experience, we tend to dismiss it as part of our imagination, thereby making it safe. Many people have a comfort zone that they are unwilling to step out of. We convince ourselves that our imagination isn't real, but what needs to be understood is that without that thought process; we couldn't breathe, eat or drink. Thought gives us the ability to create works of art, to be a leader of nations, but to every Yin there is a Yang. Thought also allows us to cause world wars and change parts of the planet beyond recognition. From this alone we can see that 'thought' is a powerful tool, so why diminish it by disbelieving it can't be used to communicate with other thought energies?

Our minds work as a whole. We don't shut our thoughts off when imagining that lottery win we've always wanted. We day dream all the time about what lives we'd like to live. I always tell my students to watch as many documentaries as they can. Spirit guides need to use thought processes that we'll understand, and the gateways to those processes are our imaginations and the information that we store there.

As we begin to trust in our imagination, it becomes more than just thinking. The thought becomes tangible. This is the starting point for the crossover from ideas, to actuality and if we merge our imaginations with our spiritual perception, there's no longer any fear that we're dealing with the unknown.

The question I'm always asked is - "How do I know that the thoughts from a guide are not my own?" Let me explain this. Thoughts that pop into the mind, without any prompting, are the first indications that it's a spiritual connection. The most important thing is not to believe that your thoughts are idle ones. If you have a thought about anything, even if it doesn't seem relevant to anything, share them with like minded friends. Or if you're already in a spiritual development group, share it with them. You'll be surprised how accurate that thought was.

Many times I've decided not to share what I was given because I thought it was of no use, only to mention it later as an afterthought and found that it was the most important message that I'd given that day. Psychic Development is your progression onto a spiritual pathway that includes progression in the physical world too. As our spiritual awareness increases, our physical life changes, usually for the better.

Some changes however, will move us on from the friend's we've known for years, or lead us back to ones we had forgotten. Whatever happens, always keep in mind that it's for the greater good and it will facilitate your journey down the avenue that you've decided to take.

As humans we've all been bestowed with free will. This means that we cannot be told what to do. Our Spirit Guides will help all they can, but if we don't listen or go off down a path to satisfy our own ego, they'll patiently wait until we return and are prepared to meet them half way again. There is no judgement, no recriminations. It's just a trusted friend waiting for you to return and acknowledge them again

Using our physic centres to receive information straight from the universal energy is a great thing, but it's not to be undertaken lightly. The contact with our spirit guides allows us to work at differing levels, preparing our minds and psyches for the next step of our spiritual evolution; it's a huge first step. Some people never want to know about their spirit guides. Yet they still spend their lives helping others. To those spiritually in the 'know' it can seem that the people in question, may not have any spiritual base, but this isn't true. The path they have chosen is no less spiritual than those who work with guides. We all have very different pathways to walk and experience.

The Spirit World and Us

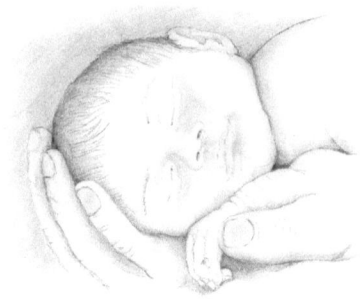

The spirit planes vibrate at an entirely different speed to the physical world. It can't be seen by the naked eye, but it can be felt and experienced by the mind. Using our psychic potential allows us to tap into the energy that surrounds us. We can see with better clarity and everything around us suddenly becomes so much more than we first thought.

The psyche is the centre of thought, feeling, and motivation. Loosely translated it means ~ mind, spirit and soul. As psychic's we are sensitive to our own energy field or Aura and therefore able to access information from the emotional, physical and spiritual parts of it. This gives us the unique ability to 'read' other people's auras and discover their real feelings and emotions. But remember, to read other peoples aura's is a great responsibility. You might not always like what you see.

Some of us can already tap into non-verbal communication such as body language, facial expressions, dress sense etc. Our first impression of someone is usually done on a psychic level. This is known as using our 'intuition' which is present from birth.

We are born into the physical world and then perceive it through our psychic abilities. A baby has a deep intuitional instinct. It knows that if it cries it will receive warmth, food and comfort. A giggle will bring it toys, attention and love. Its intuition will pick up from the auric field of a person and know instantly if that person is friendly or not. You must have heard mothers say that their baby won't take to a friend etc. This is because its intuition is telling it that the person isn't all what they seem to be.

Children often have imaginary friends. But are they really a figment of an over active mind? As they grow older, parents tell them that their imaginary friends are no longer acceptable to have. So they stop talking about them and ignore their deeper feelings because they know that they'll be chastised. This is the first stage of burying the 'psychic self'.

When people are unconsciously tapping into their psyche they say things such as 'I knew it was you calling' when they answer a telephone or they know what each other is thinking before it's even said. People can instantly know if a member of their family is ill, even though they left the house feeling fine. All these feelings and senses get us through life on a daily basis, yet these subtle influences go unnoticed because it is considered quite 'normal'.

Re-awakening Psychic ability

There are four very basic ways to reawaken our psychic abilities? But it will mean that you might need to change the way you view everything in your life.

Feel

To feel we need to re-evaluate what we do when we enter a new place. Instead of just walking in and looking idly around, you need to actually tune in your mind and 'feel' what the atmosphere around you is like. Is the temperature the same throughout the room, or does it change in certain areas? Is the air heavy or light?

What you feel about a place or person is very important. Usually your gut instincts are the right ones. Once you believe and trust in these subtle influences, they'll become easier to separate them from your everyday thoughts.

Sense

The world is ruled by the senses. Most people believe that we have five senses ~ sight, sound, taste, smell and touch. But in fact we have six. Our sixth sense. Which is our ability to receive and send information intuitively or psychically.

Intuition

The word intuition comes from the Latin word Intueri, which means to look inside. Intuition is the voice of our spirit self, sometimes called our higher self. Gut feelings, psychic powers, and spiritual insight all manifest from it. Think of it as etheric roots coming out of your feet, which draw their nourishment from the eternal ocean of universal knowledge.

Confidence in your intuition

As humans it is ingrained in us to constantly search for evidence in most things that we believe in. So having confidence in something we only feel and cannot see, is not an easy feat to undertake. Confidence comes with having belief in oneself. Once you establish this, then the rest will just fall into place.

Being Psychic v Fear

Exercise

Often when people are just developing their psychic abilities, they haven't learnt how to discern between a true vision and a picture that their ego might be creating. This causes fear to build within them and often stops them from completely understanding what is happening. Here's a very simple technique to combat this.

First of all you need to centre your mind and quieten the chatter within it. This can be achieved by doing a short, guided meditation.

Clear away any fear or negativity that might hold you back during this visualisation. Tell yourself this will be a good experience.

Now close your eyes and wait for an image to appear. It may not be instant, so please be patient.

When it forms ask yourself how did the image come to you?

Did it simply pop into your head?

Could it be related to anything you might have seen recently?

How did you feel when you saw it? Scared, happy or confused?

It's very important that you determine the source of the information from the onset. Let me give you an example to help you understand.

Pretend you're going on a trip and you are on a cruise. A gale suddenly whips up the ocean, the boat sinks and everyone dies. This is terrifying and afterwards your body races with adrenaline. But what have you really just seen?

Because the information came with an adrenaline rush of fear, it means that the scene that your mind has conjured up is connected to fears concerning a trip you might be taking. If it was a psychic vision, you would have been given the information without any emotion attached to it. You would have viewed it as though it was a movie being played out to you.

Another thing to remember is that when the mind creates a picture, the images go on and get more layered, whereas a psychic message arrives very quickly and is gone in a heartbeat. Sometimes it's possible to forget it completely. This is because it wasn't your thought to begin with.

In conclusion

If you get a spiritual image, the picture would have come from nowhere and have no emotion attached to it. The colours in it will be vibrant, but sometimes they can also be in black and white.

If an image forms solely based on your fears, you'll be very aware of it. Fear multiplies quickly and can easily create a hundred scary scenarios in a matter of seconds.

If it's an image that your ego has created your mind will be excited and fearful. Our ego likes to be a hero, so occasionally it might come up with so called psychic information to impress you.

One of best things about our intuition is that it will show us the truth of any situation. You've only got to ask. If you receive information and are not sure what to do with it, try this next visualisation:

Meditation

Find a quiet place where you will not be disturbed and sit down. Close your eyes and take three or four relaxing breaths.

Paying attention to the breath is important as it gives your mind a focus, instead of your rambling thoughts.

Focus on your solar plexus, which is around your stomach area.

Visualise a brilliant white light filling it. See the light and focus all your attention onto it.

Take another breath in through the nose, and then exhale from the mouth.

With each breath, imagine the light is getting bigger and brighter until it completely envelopes you.

Feel the peacefulness of the light. You are calm and safe here.

Now ask your inner voice if the information that came to you is accurate.

If it is, you'll get an inner knowing of yes. Be patient, you may have to ask more than once to get a reply.

Then, while continuing to focus on the light, ask if there's anything you should do about it.

If your mind starts to race with thoughts and ideas, return your focus to the calmness of the white light.

If the answer is no, you will either get a no feeling or you will feel nothing at all.

Now thank the light for guiding you and open your eyes.

Some people tell me that they aren't good at visualising and therefore cannot see the light, but I believe that everyone has an imagination. You just need to discipline yourself to use it. You need to practise, practise, and practise. Nothing worthwhile ever came easy.

Psychic Abilities

Claircognizance

Claircognizance means clear knowing.

These people have an inner knowing about things. The information just comes to them and it has a feeling of importance. They may know who is on the phone before they answer it, or know personal things about people they've just met. Many people have no idea how or why they know. There's no logic to it, no supporting evidence, it's just a deep inner feeling of knowing.

Clairaudience

Clairaudience means clear hearing.

People psychically hear sounds, words, sentences, thoughts, tones or noises that just pop into their head. They may hear conversations, footsteps or breathing just as they begin to fall asleep. These sounds and words are inaudible to the physical hearing range.

Clairvoyance

Clairvoyance means, clear seeing.

People generally see pictures flash into their minds. These can be a clear or a nebulous outlines hidden behind a wispy gauze curtain. They may see may even see a spirit person in front of them that looks as solid as they do. This spirit person can be seen just as clearly with the eyes closed, because they are being seen via the third or spiritual eye.

Please remember that when an image is of a psychic nature, it is seen first and then thought about. It's rarely thought up and then seen. A person may see scenes, objects, lights, words, colours, auras, symbols or loved ones in spirit. These pictures may appear as if you are viewing still photographs or they may be moving like a video recording.

Clairsentient

Clairsentient means Clear senses.

People perceive information through a sensation within the physical body. They may get a gut feeling as to what to do or say. They can sense pain and ill health of someone in the spirit world. They may also feel the emotions or personality of another person who has passed away.

Clairgustant

Clairgustant means clear taste

People are able to psychically taste a substance, liquid or food without actually putting anything into their mouth.

Clairiscentist

Clairiscentist means clear smelling.

People can psychically smell fragrances, flowers, perfume or other odours such as tobacco or alcohol even when it's not in their immediate surroundings that is connected to a spirit person or a past event.

Recognise your Psychic ability

Our psychic ability could be compared to a radio receiver, which in the first instance, needs to be switched on and tuned in. At this stage I must stress that in order to develop your own psychic ability to its fullest potential, you must practise continuously. There are no half way measures here. From now on when you walk into a room feel/sense the energy/atmosphere in it? This is your own psyche telling you about the room.

When you're introduced to a stranger do you form an opinion straight away of the type of person they are? How do you do this? It's your psyche speaking to you. Be aware of this information. It's never usually wrong. It's very important we understand the psyche is feeling, not seeing.

To give an example. A lady wearing a blue dress, white jacket, blue shoes and tights, is what you *see*. Without psychic potential that's all you will ever see, because your conscious mind will only acknowledge that image.

However, a psychic will *feel* what they see and the clothes will tell them more about the person. For the continuous growth of your own psychic ability you must learn to Feel, Sense and act upon your intuition.

Wake up your psychic abilities

Exercise One

Take a note pad into a café/restaurant/ park. Sit somewhere where you can study someone unobtrusively. Chose a man 60+ and a woman 30+ (separate cases, NOT a couple).

Write down about what you *feel* about each individual. Remember it's not what you *see* that matters here.

Are they sad/happy?

Do you feel they have problems?

Dig deeper into your imagination and your psychic ability will take over. It doesn't matter if you're right or wrong, the object is to start your psychic awareness flowing.

Exercise Two

Ask a friend to lend you an object to hold. In the same way a building absorbs energy, vibrations are absorbed into objects. These can be unlocked using Psychometry.

Every object has its own history to tell. It doesn't matter if you are right or wrong; say the first thing that enters your head when you hold it. Try not to analyse it first, otherwise your conscious mind will try to alter your psychic flow.

What is your first feeling?

Is the owner of the object happy or sad?

What type of person are they? Sensitive, sharp, easy going?

Relax, don't try too hard. Describe any scenes/colours/people that enter your mind.

Don't stop talking, even if you get a negative response. You can't drive a car in one day without taking many lessons, think of this as your first lesson. Ask the friend what they could understand and then write the results in your note book.

I cannot stress enough that it makes no difference if you get it wrong. This is all about waking up your psychic abilities. It is not a test for your ego to prove how good you are. Have fun with it. Let it flow into your mind. The more you enjoy the experience the easier it will get.

Tapping into the Psyche

We need to recognise our psychic ability. To do that we have to examine our lifestyle and the responsibility our psychic skills will place on us.

To work with our psychic centres we must be in a calm and relaxed state of mind and body. If we're emotionally or physically out of balance, or taking any form of drugs, our psychic abilities will become clouded and what we feel and sense will not be correct. So firstly, we need to ask our self — what do we hope to achieve by developing our psychic ability? Is it to help others, ourselves, or do we just have that a deep yearning of just wanting to know? This will help us to understand why we are walking on this particular pathway.

Our whole body is attuned to vibration. Because everything that lives, vibrates with its own unique frequency. The vibrations we pick up goes on to link us to our intuition. We've mostly learnt over the years to trust our feelings. But now we need to learn to differentiate between them and our intuition.

To break down what emotions are, you need to think of them as a chemical by-product of our thoughts. Sometimes they can be very loud. This is because they are designed to draw our attention and override our intuition. To fight this daily distraction we must become more aware that our intuition is trying to help us. Eventually, the more we set our intention to listen, the more we'll hear it. We must be stubborn about this and work on it. Because one day that intuition could save your life.

Meditation is a great way to develop our intuition. This is because during the meditation process, we release stress and quieten the chatter within us. Behind the constant activity of our minds is the peace of intuition. We just need to find it.

The word intuition comes from the Latin word intueri. Translated, it means to look inside or to contemplate. As we developed in the modern world, a choice was made to make science our way of life. This decision was really the end for us using our intuition as a basis for navigating through life. Science accused those who used their psychic ability of being delusional, unstable, or liars. This egotistical labelling caused many of us to dismiss our gut instincts and leave ourselves open to danger and outside influences.

How does intuition work?

Your chakras, or energy centres, have a particular kind of intuition associated with them. When the consciousness associated with the chakras become clear, they open and the intuition becomes active. Divine knowledge is in us all. It just needs to be activated.

The root chakra, the source of our kinaesthetic sense, allows us to acknowledge sensations such as shivers down our spine, hairs standing up on end or a change of room temperature.

The sacral chakra, located just below the navel, is empathy. This allows us to feel another's emotions. If we want to develop empathy, it's important to be closely in touch with our own emotions. Otherwise, someone else's emotions will become hard to distinguish from our own. If we continue to be calm and grounded when we embark on this journey, our balanced body will eventually recognise these are not our own feelings and reassert itself.

The solar plexus chakra's, located in the stomach area, is our subtle sense - true intuition. This is when we get that vague feeling that something's about to happen. Unfortunately, it comes with no details. That's where trusting what you feel is right comes into sharp focus.

The heart chakra's attunement is to love and relationships. Relationships create happiness. A vital part of our physical health and well-being that also resonates with our spirit.

The fifth chakra, the throat, is the source of creativity and sound-related intuition. When this is active, you'll be able to tune into spiritual guidance.

The sixth chakra, third eye, located in the centre of the forehead, gives us the ability to see energy patterns, images, and spiritual visions. Don't be surprised if they disappear as soon as you've seen them. Ignore the impulse to believe that you made it up. Remember your thoughts will always try to distract you.

The seventh chakra, crown, is on the top of the head and is where direct knowing is formed. It's similar to a feeling of recognition that you just can't put your finger on.

How can we find our Intuition?

The intuition lies above the rational mind and below the spirit dimension. Here lies a plane of consciousness called the Intuitional; it's also known as the sub-conscious mind. It feels responses, images and shapes, and physical manifestations, as clearly as we would feel a physical touch. But don't get confused here. Our Intuition has nothing to do with emotional feelings, which inform us how we feel regarding situations or relationships. For example, our emotions might tell us that we are very attracted to someone and they're worth getting to know better. While our intuition is screaming—NO—are you mad!!!

Intuitive feelings are not always logical, but they are incredibly informative. It would be an error to ignore them as the intuition perceives the vibrations of consciousness outside the mind by using psychic perception. In other words, it knows better than you what is right and wrong.

We need to convince our mind to listen to our intuitive feelings and value them. It's not possible to just pretend at this. The mind is rational. It requires an acceptable reason to accept psychic feelings as a valid one. So we need to start to introduce the mind to where these feelings come from.

Ask yourself: Where does my psychic information come from?

Why should I listen to it?

Is it trustworthy?

Am I comfortable tuning in to it?

Believe it or not the answer received will be very specific.

The feelings we receive are often subtle. So if our life is very busy, intuitive feelings will be almost impossible to recognise. So how can we recognise it? It's quite simple really. A quiet room in the house, where you will not be disturbed, is all that's needed. Set a specific time to connect, as this one act of intention subconsciously tells the body that it's okay to relax.

Sit comfortably, preferably upright and not lying down.

Start to still your mind from its endless chatter and focus your thoughts inwards.

Become aware of what is happening inside of you. Give yourself permission to think only about yourself for a change.

Find your intuition

First of all we need to realise that when this meditation of self-discovery is followed, we may feel nothing within the physical body. This usually means there is an emotional blockage within us. We don't want to feel, so our mind acknowledges that as a type of silent command. If this does occur, ask yourself why don't you want to feel? It takes practice to ask this question, because a lot of the time we will block out the response. But please do persevere.

To do this meditation takes great courage because we are looking inwards at ourselves and we, as humans, are rarely happy with what we find. If you do feel this way, it's a good idea to learn to heal yourself through meditation. It's hard to let go of hurt, fear and anger. But let go we must, as they serve no purpose but to hold us back from progressing in life. To help others, we must first help our self. Once this is acknowledged the aches and pains inside our body can begin to be released. You don't need to do this alone. A good Crystal Therapist can use various crystal remedies to help you with this journey.

A good affirmation is 'I ask Archangel Michel to cut the ties that bind me to any negative emotions.'

Then: I call upon Archangel Chamuel to heal the wounds left behind by people and situations that do not nurture my spirit in any way.

Meditation

I want you to concentrate on what you are feeling in different parts of your body.

So with your feet on the floor and your hands on your lap, close your eyes.

Take a deep breath in through the nose and exhale through the mouth.

Slow down your breathing ~ there's no rush ~ you have all the time in the world.

Do this four times.

Focus on nothing but the breath going into the body and then leaving it.

If your mind begins to wander, acknowledge that it's done it and then bring it back to concentrate on your breath.

Focus on attention on your abdomen.

Take yourself to it. Feel that you are there. What do you feel in that area? Is it heavy ~ light ~ bloated?

Remember this feeling.

Move on to your chest. Is it tight ~ loose ~ heavy? Make it comfortable by telling whatever you feel to go away.

Your upper legs? Is there tension there? If so tell them to relax. Give them permission.

Is there confusion in other parts of your body? OR is there nothing?

Remember these feelings as you concentrate again on your breath.

Bring your mind back to the breath.

When you are ready, open your eyes.

This meditation will help you to focus on self-healing all of your body. Go to every part of your body; make up your own guided mediation. The picture in this section of the bluebells is an excellent tool to meditate with. Imagine you are on that pathway, walking through the flowers. Ask your spiritual helpers to help with the words that you will need to heal yourself.

Remember, Intuition comes from the spirit. We are not supposed to be on the physical earth wandering aimlessly through our life. We are born with a particular agenda and our intuition will be trying to keep us in alignment with that. We need to practise using our intuition every day. NEVER think at this stage that it's unimportant. We must instil into our sub-conscious mind the techniques for awakening our psychic potential.

You will know when this endless practising reaches its fruition, because when the intuition starts to become stronger any dreams will become more vivid. Everything about us begins to change on a subtle level. We start to love the world and ourselves. It is an exciting journey. Full of wonder and happiness. We are not designed to be weak, egotistical, warmongering, selfish, vain creatures. But this is what we might become if we decide to ignore our true self.

There is a state of mind whilst we are dreaming called Hypnogogic dreaming. This usually occurs just before we fall into the Delta state of sleep. Which is the deep sleep that we struggle to wake up from. Recognise this state of mind as it will help to develop the intuitive thoughts further. It's quite possible to make this sleep state work for us. Here's how.

Before closing your eyes, focus your attention on a subject you wish to dream about. As you become sleepy, try to stay awake for as long as you can. You should see pictures, images in your mind's eye. Try to remember them. Now wake yourself from the brink of sleep and write down what you saw.

Some people, by practising this exercise, have managed, through intuition, to predict future events. Don't expect to get success on the first try though. It takes many years of self-discipline to train the mind to this extent. Our intuition isn't based on what we consider may be right or wrong. Practising using it allows us to use our senses to come to a conclusion.

Here are a few exercises you need to start practising on a regular basis.

Exercise One

Write down what you 'feel' those close to you are experiencing today. Your partner, son, daughter, friend etc. Do you feel they're happy, sad, etc.? What kind of mood are they in?

Exercise Two

What kind of atmosphere is present in your home today? Sense it, feel it, recognise it. Be guided by your intuition as you write.

Exercise Three

From today as you speak to people, 'feel' them, sense the energies emanating from them. Soon it'll become second nature to do this and people thoughts will become easier to read.

DO NOT at this stage divulge to anyone you have tuned into, any intuitive thoughts you may have about them.

Write it down and keep it safe. The more you practise this simple exercise, the more you'll begin to stir up your psychic energies.

Exercise Four

Tune into places you visit. I.E shops offices, hotels. Feel the energy in the room. If you feel something may happen in or at this place, write it down.

I said earlier that we are like a radio waiting to be tuned into the right station. Now we need to learn how to tune ourselves in. As our psychic ability develops, gut feeling or intuitive thought about anything, at this stage need to be kept to our self. This is part of a self-discipline regime that must be adhered to if development is to be kept in a controlled manner.

Understanding the energy of the body

We have already discussed 'feeling and sensing'; now we need to know how to convert what we see into these two actions. As human beings we go through life with our eyes wide open, but how many of us actually 'see' what's around us? Every living thing, right down to a dandelion weed, has its own unique energy pattern. Think of it as a type of DNA signature. Crowds generate an enormous amount of energy, so concerts will always be heaving with vibrational energy. You don't need psychic skills to feel the crackle of excitement in the air. This is known as group energy, where everyone is contributing even though they have no idea that they are doing it.

Many spiritual development circles are called 'closed circles'. This means only a selected few can participate, making the circle quite spiritually powerful. Each member is adding their energy to the whole group on a regular basis. Now the individual's vibration starts to become part of a whole.

People who participate in circle's go on to develop close friendships. This is because they are blending with each other. They trust the people they are with because they can literally 'see' them through the eyes of their intuition. A good development circle is only as good as the people in it. The teacher/leader may be brilliant, but if the group energy doesn't unite, the circle will not flourish as it should. There needs to be commitment from every individual to attend. When this starts to falter, the whole dynamics of the circle will crumble.

The following exercise will give you a unique chance to experience group energy

Go to a library. The atmosphere in these places is usually calm and relaxed, so perfect for you to practise in. Sit down and tune into someone's energy. Look at them and see how you feel about what they are feeling.

Happy, sad or anxious?

What are they wearing?

What do the clothes colours tell you about them?

Write in your notebook everything that you sense and feel about this person. Don't try too hard. Let your mind relax and focus on this individual. Spend some time doing this with other people who are there.

The more you practise, the more proficient you will become.

The Aura

The Aura is an amazing part of us. It is our life force, the energy vibrations that map out who we really are. It's the shape of an ellipse ~ think egg shape ~ and encompasses our whole body. It's powered by the chakras, our spiritual energy centres. They obtain their energy from the life force that rises from the earth and descends from the sky, entering our bodies from all different directions through the hundreds of tiny chakras within our body. When someone is listening to music, their aura changes to match the vibrations of the sound and harmony.

The aura is made up of seven different layers. The outer ones are concerned with the soul and spirit while the inner layers relate to the mind, emotions and health. People who are gifted with clairvoyance can see it very clearly. Colours flash around the body at different speeds, highlighting how that person is feeling or reacting to their environment.

Healers can sometimes spot illness in the auric field before it manifests physically. It will show up as dark spots or holes. Many things can affect the aura in a negative way. Arguments, computers, trauma or serious illness are but a few. Taking care of our aura is paramount. It's a huge part of us and if it's out of balance, it can make our lives miserable. We cannot fake the Aura. It shows who we are, what our true intentions are.

Every living thing has an aura. Every thought, feeling and experience affects the vibration of this amazing energy field. Children can see auras very clearly. Hence the blue cows and green sheep they draw when young. They're probably seeing the predominant colour emanating from the animals aura.

The Aura can tell us many things about ourselves; that's why it's so important to get to know it. Expanding away from our bodies to about an arm's length, the aura can vary in size according to our moods and current health. The colours may vary in shade, but there are only seven rainbow colours vibrating within it.

Seeing the Aura

Because an aura extends outwards, we don't have to stare at a person to see it. Look slightly to the right of them, close the eyes and then open them slowly and blink. In that single moment we will see one predominant colour. This is the mood aura. What that person's really feeling. When we do this we are bringing an aspect of the person into sharper focus. If this doesn't happen straight away, practise. Remember, your logical mind will always try to intercede and tell you that what you see isn't true. It's up to you to quell its chatter and make it silent. Most people will see the aura as a misty haze. This is because the subtle energy pulsates and shifts constantly around us at various speeds.

Exercise One

Sit in front of a mirror. There should be a soft light illuminating you and the room. Make sure the background behind you is plain in colour. Be sure the light does not reflect in the mirror. Release all preconceptions of what you think your aura will look like. When you see a colour do not discredit it. You're reading the aura intuitively, so trust your impressions.

Look at yourself in the mirror, slightly to one side, not full on. Allow the eyes to go out of focus, as if you were looking beyond your body's reflection. This shifts your brainwaves from Beta (everyday thinking) to the Theta state of consciousness, because the aura is seen first with the mind's eye, and then with the physical eyes.

Usually, the first layer of the aura is seen ~ Etheric. It appears as a light gray or a wispy haze about an inch above the skin surface. Colours are easiest seen around the head. Practice doing this and eventually you will be amazed to see the colours we have vibrating around us.

To feel the electromagnetic energies coming from our body, hold the palms of the hand facing each other—about two inches apart. Wait a few seconds. You'll feel a tingling sensation or something pushing gently between your hands. Once you begin to feel the sensation of electromagnetic energies between your palms, move them slowly to and fro. You'll feel the movement of your aura. Try moving your palms slowly further and further apart. See how far you can go before you no longer feel the 'pull'. Remember to check periodically by moving your hands slightly.

It's quite possible to have experienced someone's auric field and not known. For instance, when we are with a certain person is there a sense of feeling drained when they have gone? Remember the feeling of being stared at, yet no one is there? Has there ever been a time when you just know how a person is feeling just by looking at them? If this has been experienced we have felt/sensed someone else's aura.

As we get to know our aura, we'll know what needs topping up in it. This can be done by using a coloured crystal or eating the colour we need in food. To give an example: An orange will top up the energy lacking in the sacral chakra. To give your whole aura a boost, go to the park, sea or woodland. Anywhere there is nature. Let the natural colours soak into the aura. People feel so much better after going to the seaside. Why? Because the ocean positively vibrates with life and energy. The aura will soak it up, leaving the body sated, calm and in perfect balance.

We are all spiritual beings in a physical body. The earth's energy is our spiritual food, without it we would wither and die. The more vibrant the rainbow is within us, the more healthy and balanced we will become.

Aura colour guide and meanings

Red

Relates to the physical body, heart or circulation. The densest colour, it creates the most friction, which can attract or repel; money worries or obsessions; anger or forgivingness, anxiety or nervousness.

Deep Red: Grounded, realistic, active, strong will-power, survival-oriented.

Muddied Red: Anger (repelling)

Clear red: Powerful, energetic, competitive, sexual, and passionate.

Pink-bright and light: Loving, tender, sensitive, sensual, artistic, affection, purity, compassion; new or revived romantic relationship. Can indicate clairaudience.

Dark and murky pink: Immature and/or dishonest nature.

Orange Red: Confidence, creative power. In a good, bright and pure state, red energy can be a sign of a healthy ego

Yellow

Relates to reproductive organs and emotions. The colour of vitality, vigour, good health and excitement. Lots of energy and stamina, creative, productive, adventurous, courageous, outgoing social nature; currently experiencing stress related to appetites and addictions.

Orange-Yellow: Creative, intelligent, detail oriented, perfectionist, scientific. Relates to the spleen and life energy. It's the colour of awakening, inspiration, intelligence and action shared, creative, playful, optimistic, and easy-going.

Light or pale yellow: Emerging psychic and spiritual awareness; optimism and hopefulness; positive excitement about new ideas.

Bright lemon-yellow: Struggling to maintain power and control in a personal or business relationship; fear of losing control, prestige, respect, and/or power.

Clear gold metallic, shiny and bright: Spiritual energy and power activated and awakened; an inspired person.

Dark brownish yellow or gold: A student or one who is straining at studying; overly analytical to the point of feeling fatigued or stressed; trying to make up for "lost time" by learning everything all at once.

Blue

Relates to the throat, thyroid. It is the colour of calm and quietness. Caring, loving, intuitive.

Soft blue: Peacefulness, clarity and communication.

Bright royal blue: Clairvoyant; highly spiritual nature; generous; on the right path.

Dark or muddy blue: Fear of the future; fear of self-expression; fear of facing or speaking the truth

The muddier shades of blue can reflect blocked perceptions. They can indicate melancholy, fearfulness and over sensitivity.

Orange

Reflects warmth, creativity and emotions. It is an indication of courage.

Depending on the shade, it can also indicate emotional imbalances and agitation. Some of the muddier shades of orange can reflect pride and flamboyance.

Green

Relates to heart and lungs. It's a very comfortable, healthy colour of nature. When seen in the aura this usually represents growth and balance. Love of people, animals, nature; teacher.

Bright emerald green: A healer, also a love-centred person.

Yellow-Green: Creative with heart. Dark or muddy forest green: Jealousy, resentment, feeling like a victim of the world; blaming self or others; insecurity and low self-esteem.

Pink

Pink is a colour of compassion, love and purity. When seen in the aura, it can indicate the quiet, modest type of individual, along with a love of art and beauty.

Depending on the shade of pink, it can also reflect an immaturity, a lack of truthfulness. It can also reflect times of new love and new vision.

Purple

Relates to crown, pineal gland and nervous system. The most sensitive and wisest of colours. This is the intuitive colour in the aura, and reveals psychic power of attunement with self. Intuitive, visionary, futuristic, idealistic, artistic, magical.

Lavender: Imagination, visionary, daydreamer. It is the colour of warmth and transmutation. The paler and lighter shades reflect humility and spirituality.

The red-purple shades can indicate great passion and strength of will.

Muddier shades can reflect a need to overcome something. The person has a tendency to be overbearing, needing sympathy and feeling misunderstood.

Gold

Gold is an eighth colour rarely seen. It a very powerful colour found in only the most spiritual of people and it means the person has a close connection to the divine. It reflects the higher energies of devotion and great inspiration.

Other colours sometimes seen

Black

Draws or pulls energy to it and in so doing, transforms it. It captures light and consumes it. Usually indicates long-term un-forgiveness towards others. If it collects in a specific area of the body, it can lead to health problems; Past life hurts; unreleased grief from abortions if it appears in the ovaries.

White

Reflects other energy. A pure state of light. Often represents a new, not yet designated energy in the aura. Spiritual, etheric and non-physical qualities, transcendent, higher dimensions. Purity and truth; angelic qualities.

White sparkles or flashes of white light: angels are nearby; can indicate that the person is pregnant or will be soon.

Rainbows

Rainbow-coloured stripes, sticking out like sunbeams from the hand, head or body: A Reiki healer, or a star person ~ someone who is in the first incarnation on Earth.

The Aura shape

The aura shape and colours within are very important. The aura's spiralling colour vibration field can be seen, felt, and interpreted in an aura reading. Should a colour or colours in it need healing, an aura healing can take place, bringing it back into balance.

A well-balanced aura should be centred all the way around, with the colours' stability being carefully paid attention to. An aura healer will check for breaks, gaps, or holes as well as the intensity of the colour within it. The auric energy field not only goes around you, but moves within your body as well. It's not just the outside of your body that's made of electromagnetic energies.

The Aura vibrates with colour and this can change in accordance with a person's emotional, mental, and spiritual states. Holes are due to the electromagnetic energies suddenly stopping. They are often seen as black holes or grey patches. These imbalances will cause a direct reaction in the physical body, causing symptoms such as depression, anxiety or panic attacks.

An Aura healer senses blockages and areas within the energy field that are not functioning properly. A good one will be able to detect diseases in their advanced stages that may require immediate medical attention. This is because sometimes the aura becomes infected long before it manifests physically. Healers work on balancing the aura energy fields so that the aura colours are brighter and in harmony with each other. When everything's in balance, physical health, emotions and spiritual peace is attained.

Aura healers use many techniques to refocus the aura. Some of them include Aura Awareness, Chakra Balancing, Chi – Ki – Qi, Distant Healing, Grounding, Pranic Healing, Reiki, Vaastu and Yuen Method. A popular technique used is called Auric-Soma. This is a colour and light therapy that works through the colour spectrum and its various frequencies.

Layers of the aura

1. Physical body - Physical sensations and health.

2. The Etheric body - Brings together all the lower chakras; acupuncture meridians are the energetic lines of this body. Governs emotions with respect to self.

3. Inner astral body - The link between soul and matter; the silver cord that binds the spirit to the physical body.

4. Psychic body - Where the ego dwells.

5. Spiritual body – This brings together all the higher chakras. Every thought that you have will draw a line of energy into this body.

6. Divine body - The spiritual potential is linked with the energy of this body.

7. Astral body - That part of us that is connected the universe or divine source.

It's possible to cleanse the aura using crystals or essential oils. Frankincense being the best high vibrational oil to use. Put a small amount in your palms, rub them together then swipe your hands around your body.

Crystals should be only used by an experienced therapist as they harness a wealth of power and can be dangerous if not used wisely. Meditation is very important if we want to become attuned to ourselves. In this state of consciousness, we can self-heal our body. It's useful to practice this basic aura meditation on a daily basis. Our awareness of energy can build on this foundation of grounding and balancing the aura.

Aura **Meditation**

Look at the picture of the fields and allow your body to relax as you do so. Imagine that you are sitting on the lush grass. The day is warm, the sun is shining. Now visualise a grounding cord of energy between your hips and the centre of the planet... Let your cord have a steady downward flow of energy... Use it to release any excess energy out of your system... Any hurt, pain, anger, any negative emotions that hold you back in life... Give yourself permission to let them go... Be mindful of your breath... I want you to take a deep breath in through the nose and out through the mouth... gently... there's no rush... do this four times in slow controlled breaths. Now be aware of the centre of your head... Imagine yourself picking up a tiny chair and placing it in the centre of your head... You're so tiny... A small extension of yourself... Sit down on the chair... Relax... continue with your breaths... If you're still thinking a lot, you're too far forward... move back into the centre of your head... Sit in the quiet... relax... this is your sacred space... nothing can harm you here....

Begin to open up your awareness of the field of energy around your physical body... Notice if your energy is closed in tight around your body, or spread out far away from your body... This is your aura... Your energy field... Mentally begin to draw your aura inwards until it is about an arm's length around your body... Draw your aura in at the back... left and right sides... above your head and below your feet... Wrap yourself in your own energy at arm's length all the way around you... Notice what it feels like... Be aware of yourself as a spiritual being, made of energy... Your aura is your personal space... No one may enter this space without your permission... Keep releasing any excess or unwanted energy down to the centre of the earth through your cord... When you feel ready... centred and relaxed... take a few deep breaths... slowly open your eyes, and begin to move... Notice how you feel after doing the aura meditation exercise.

Energy from objects

Psychometry

The term Psychometry was first used in the mid-nineteenth century by Joseph R. Buchanan, an American physiologist. It's interpreting the energy of an object to obtain information about its history and/or owner. Sometimes the energy of the person who owned the item is left behind and it's possible to tune into it.

To start you need to quieten your mind from all its chatter. Concentrate on a one word mantra, such as peace, love, intention any word that keeps you focused and do a short meditation.

Exercise

Take an object from a friend. It doesn't matter what it is, and place it on a table in front of you. Relax and study it. Sense and feel its energy. There's no rush, take your time.

Speak about how you feel about the object.

How old do you feel it is?

Where has it been?

Is it warm or cold?

See how much you can get right. Remember, you're practising, so don't get too despondent if you don't always get it right.

It's good to buy some old bric-a-brac from a charity shop and practise. There's no wrong way to do this. All you're doing is honing your psychic skills. It's beneficial for your psychic development, to do this exercise at least once a day. Psychic intuition by itself is insufficient. You need to learn to interpret energy into psychic visions accurately in order to develop properly. I can't reiterate enough to practise. It's the key to unlocking all your skills.

Chakras

Crown - Spiritual

3rd Eye - Perception

Throat - Expression

Heart - Love

Solar Plexus - Power

Sacral - Sex

Root - Survival

It's important at this stage of psychic development that we learn about our chakras. These are our inner, energy wheels, invisible to the naked eye, but just as important to us as the breath that gives us life. Chakra is a Sanskrit word meaning wheel, or vortex, and it refers to the seven centres of which the body's energy system is composed of.

These were first described over 2,500 years ago, in ancient sacred texts. The seven chakras are the root, spleen, solar plexus, heart, throat, brow, and crown. These energy centres regulate the flow of energy within us, just as the heart regulates the blood. Because Chakras are not physical organs, many people refuse to acknowledge their existence. It really draws our attention back again to the fact of how narrowed our perception of the body has become over the centuries.

Chakras do not contain energy; instead when we need it, the energy is automatically drawn up from the planet by the minor chakras in the legs and feet. It then flows through the body depositing energy into the main chakra system. We love to run around with bare feet? Especially on the beach or grass? Why? Because our chakras gain energy from the body's direct contact with the earth. It revitalises us without us even realising what's happening. Our body is intuitively telling us what it needs and we are responding even though we have no idea we are doing it.

If we could see the chakras they would look like spinning wheels of vibrant colour. Each one has its own designated frequency. They are attached to the spinal cord and nervous system via certain glands and nerve ganglia. As the body chakra system is quite complex, the best way to describe it is to break it down into stages.

There are three masters, four major and over 300 minor chakras. Outside the body there are even more. Eastern medicine has been using the meridians that connect them for thousands of years. Acupuncture being the most well-known. When the chakras are in perfect balance, a person will feel healthy and full of vitality.

The chakras interact with the physical body through two major vehicles: the endocrine system and the nervous system. Each of the seven chakras is associated with one of the seven endocrine glands, and also with a group of nerves called a plexus. They represent not only particular parts of our physical body, but also particular parts of our consciousness.

When we feel tension, it will be felt in the chakras. Where we feel stress depends upon why we feel it. The tension in the chakra is detected by the nerves of the plexus and transmitted to the parts of the body controlled by it. If the tension isn't resolved and continues, the person will go on to manifest a symptom on a physical level. Sicknesses in the stomach, panic attacks, are all signs of stress related feelings.

Once we begin to understand our chakra system, we will then go forward and understand the relationship between the consciousness and the body.

The seven main chakras

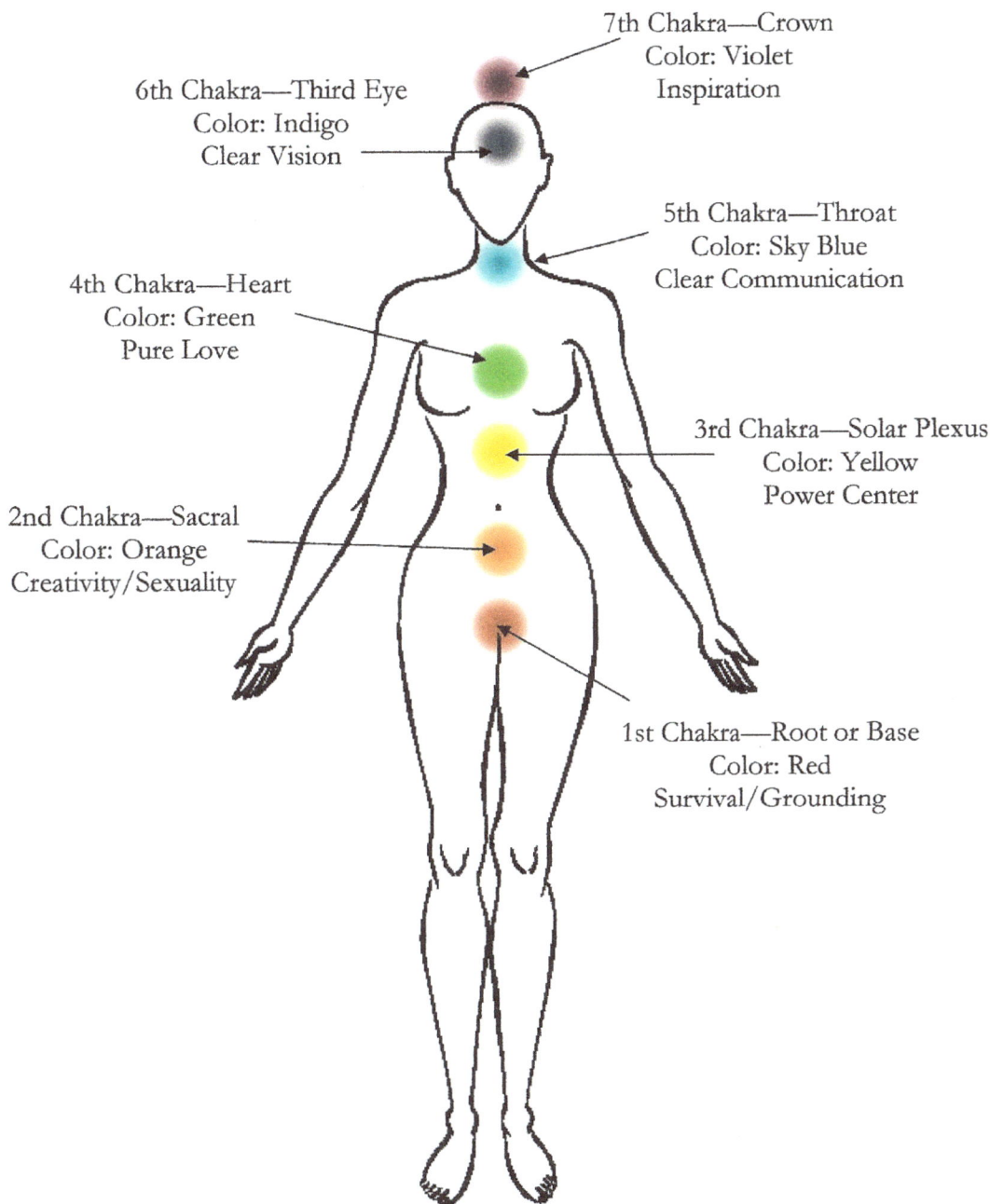

1st Chakra ~ Root

The Root chakra is found at the base of the spine. It connects our body to the spirit, aiding our everyday survival. From the root we get our physical energy and good health. Throughout the ancient world, the root chakra has been associated with dragons and snakes. It is the centre that harbours Kundalini fire. The most powerful energy a human can have. This energy lies dormant in most of people, with only a few, deeply connected spiritual people, being able to harness its full power.

Its colour varies in shade. From dark red to light.

2nd Chakra ~ Sacral

The sacral is found in the lower abdomen, just below the navel. Our creativity resides here, along with any life and death decisions that we make. Emotions and the hunger for self-gratification all manifest within this chakra. The sacral supports the sexual organs, intestine, and bladder, and is connected to the lumbar spine area.

This chakra helps you to learn how to make your own reality and can be affected by emotions such as love, fear and hate.

Its colour is orange of various shades.

3rd Chakra ~ Solar Plexus

The solar plexus can be found midway between the navel and the base of the ribs. The solar plexus supports the spleen, pancreas, stomach, and liver. When balanced, the digestive system works exceptionally well. It is here that our self-esteem is defined and our Gut feeling originates.

Its colour is deep yellow.

4th Chakra ~ Heart

The heart chakra can be found in the centre of the chest. This is a very important energy centre as it is the point of balance for all the chakras. It supports the physical heart, thymus gland, lower lung, and circulatory system, and governs relationships and how we interact with other people. A well-balanced heart chakra leads to expansion and growth on a physical level.

We use this chakra to connect with those we love. Whether that is for a human being or an animal. Once forged, these links are hard to break and this explains why we suffer so much through the break-up of a relationship or the loss of a loved one. The heart chakra maintains peace within us which then spins out to all the other chakras.

Its colour is green with a pink centre.

5th Chakra ~ Throat

The throat chakra resides in the throat. It supports the mouth, ears, thyroid gland, arms, and hands. From this centre we speak our truth or lies and it is also the rainbow bridge from which we pass from the physical to the spiritual realm.

Its colour is blue.

6th Chakra ~ Brow

The brow chakra is found between the centre of the eyebrows and it supports the carotid artery, brain, neurological system, eyes, ears, nose, pituitary and pineal glands. It's the level of consciousness that directs our actions and lives. Commonly known as the third eye, this chakra is where we connect to God's consciousness and get spirit-to-spirit communication

7th Chakra ~ Crown

The crown chakra is found on the top of the head. This is where you enter and exit the physical body as a spirit evolving through endless lives. It has the highest energy of all the chakras and connects us to our universal oneness. It supports the skull, cerebral cortex, skin, right brain, right eye, and the nervous, muscular, and skeletal systems.

This chakra is depicted as a lotus flower with a hundred petals, and when opened fully a highly polished diamond crystal rests in the centre of it. When visualised opening, it brings immense spiritual energy to the person. It supports our values, morals, and ethics, and is the gateway to our higher consciousness. Here the laws of the universe are understood.

Its colour is luminous violet, reaching up to the brilliant white. It is known as the pure light of god.

A Chakra Meditation

The picture above has distinct colours, look at it and see what colour attracts you. This will deter mine what chakra needs energy. Before any spiritual meditation is undertaken it's important you ask for protection from the spirit world.

Find a place where there will be no disturbances, light a white candle, sit down, close your eyes and say a little prayer. Here is an example, but anything from the heart made be spoken.

Heavenly father, divine spirit, I ask that my guides and helpers draw close to me and place me in a protective bubble of one hundred per cent pure, white light. I ask that they help me with anything that I need to do with my life's purpose and any spiritual work that I may perform today. Amen.

Meditate on the picture above for a few minutes, while your mind stills and the chatter ceases.

Meditation

Please note that this chakra meditation can be bought at Margaret West's website www.connectionswithspirit.co.uk

When you are comfortable, close your eyes and take a deep breath in through your nose, hold this for a few seconds and then exhale through your mouth. (Repeat about three times.)

Feel the air fill your lungs, and as it does, pay attention to your feet.

Visualise dark brown roots coming from your feet. See them push through the floor and then embed themselves in the soft welcoming earth.

Feel the heaviness in your legs as they firmly anchor your feet to the floor.

Now visualise a white light pushing up from the floor. It moves through your feet, calves, thighs, up to your torso, arms, hands and fingers; feel this energy course through your body and feel it begin to relax you.

Make sure you stay aware of how your body is feeling.

The light is now up to your shoulders, you're feeling the tension ebb away, it moves up to your head.

Relax. Nothing should bother you now. You're safe and secure in your sacred space.

Now visualise at the base of your spine a dull, red light.

Now visualise that light becoming bright and vibrant.

Move up to just below your navel. See a dull, orange light.

Visualise this light becoming bright and vibrant.

Move up to the area just above your navel and see a dull, yellow light.

Visualise it bright and vibrant.

Move up to the centre of your chest. See a dull, green light.

Visualise it bright and vibrant.

Move up to the throat. See a dull, blue light,

Visualise it bright and vibrant.

Move up to the brow and visualise a dull violet light.

Visualise it bright and vibrant.

Move up the crown. See a tight, white bud, but it is bigger than any you have ever seen. Visualise it opening into a lotus flower of brilliant white.

Take a deep breath through your nose and exhale through your mouth and when you are ready, open your eyes.

Your chakras are now open, which means you are open for psychic work.

Closing the Chakras

Before we can carry on with our daily life it is important we close the chakras that we have opened to connect with the spirit world. DO NOT be complacent about this. After all, we wouldn't go out and leave our front door open for anyone to just stroll in, so why leave ourselves wide open for other people's negativity to flood in.

To close the chakras the meditation for opening them can be done in reverse. Just visualise the vibrant lights going back to being dull again. Always start at your base chakra ~ Root.

Having now obtained the ability to tune in to the higher consciousness, our psyche has now begun to awaken. This ability, inherent in us all, can now be now be used to benefit others as well as ourselves.

Psychic Development is NOT fortune telling. This amazing journey is a serious undertaking and must not be treated lightly. As we follow the pathway that is set for us on this spiritual journey of enlightenment, friends may approach us more with their problems. Strangers will become friendlier and chat with us. Why? Because our spiritual light is switched on and is now beaming love and light into the universe and into the spirit of others that we meet.

Meditation

Throughout this book we have spoken about meditation and how it can facilitate the altered state that we need to place our minds into. Some people love it and take to it well, others are not so lucky. It's hard to shut everything out that makes our minds tic over at lightning speed for most of the day. But to be able to successfully continue on this Psychic Development journey, it's important we learn how to quieten our minds. In this modern age most people think the best way to relax is in front of the television. This may be beneficial to some, but we need to ask ourselves what part of this nourishes our mind and spirit?

Meditation is a state of mind. It is a way to calm your thoughts. Whether you are a man or a woman, both male and female energies co-exist within your body. Balancing them is an important aspect of the meditation process. This is because the male energy is predominantly concerned with action and the female with intuition. If these become out of balance it means that we are not gaining benefit from either.

The picture above is designed to work in a soothing way on the senses. There is nothing much going on in it to focus the mind on, yet the colours are soothing. As we stare into its depths the mind will become quite still.

So let's look deeper into meditation and how we can use it to benefit ourselves.

There are two main types of meditation.

Concentrative Meditation

Practitioners of Yoga and meditation believe that there is a direct link between the breath and our state of mind. If a person is anxious or fearful, the breath tends to be shallow, rapid, and uneven. But when the mind is calm and composed, the breath is slow, deep, and regular. Focusing the mind on the continuous rhythm of breathing in and out gives the mind something to do. The chatter within begins to still and we find that meditative state we've been searching for.

Mindfulness Meditation

This involves opening up our attention to the continuous parade of sensations, images, thoughts, sounds, and smells, without actually becoming involved in thinking about them. Just sit quietly and acknowledge whatever goes through the mind, not reacting or becoming involved with the thoughts or images. This way we gain a greater sense of calm and our mind no longer reacts. So unlike concentrative meditation, where the sight is narrowed to a selected field, here we are the entire field.

Keeping the right balance

There are hundreds of ways of getting to a meditative state. Everyone will eventually be drawn to a way that works best for them. When we make a conscious decision to meditate, especially alone, it's a good idea to protect ourselves against any untoward energy that maybe lurking. This can be done is a number of ways. Visualise yourself in a pink bubble or in a tube of white light, are two ideas.

At any time during a meditation there is a feeling of disquiet, stop! The person meditating has the control here. Understand that meditation fine tunes our visualisation capabilities. We are asking to be touched by spirit in some form or other. So the mind needs to be focussed, without distractions or interruptions. We create our own realities. Each thought we have is us being creative. We use imagery and feelings in all aspects of our everyday life. If I was to ask a person to imagine an apple, it would probably be seen as red and crispy. But that's all they'd see if they are just picturing it. But, if the subject is visualising the apple, it would slowly begin to change. A stem would appear, leaves would magically grow; maybe a branch where it hangs from would form. This is because other thoughts are being layered over the top of the original one about the apple.

Practise is the key to success. We have to understand our own method of seeing, and then test it for accuracy. This is why the mind must be alert during a meditation. The only thing relaxing should be the body. Never lie down, as this is called the 'prone' position and induces sleep. Sit straight, so you chakras are aligned and ready to work. Choose an upright chair. Don't make it too comfortable otherwise it will cause the body to slump. Remember, nothing can hurt us during these visualisations. We always have full control over them.

A group meditation is far more powerful, as are the healing energies generated there. The collective energy of members and those in spirit are magnified many times. There are many reasons for this. One reason being that while a circle forms on the physical plane, another forms in spirit and then a group forms around the spirit one and so on an so forth, creating endless circles of energy. Groups, who meditate in a set place and at a set time, become attuned quickly to the build-up of energy that is almost waiting for them. The vibrations of the people present and the energy from spirit naturally harmonise. Protection is also less of a problem here as a regular group meeting generates a protected circle of light around it.

It's very important to remember that whenever we work with spirit energies, the pure white light that comes to us will also attract darker energy. It's always a good idea to say a small protection prayer when we open ourselves to the etheric realms. Eventually it'll become second nature. Remember, that as well as messages coming through from spirit, that we can understand, they will also come through using words, which the person for whom it is intended for, will only understand. We, as facilitators, don't need to fully understand a message as it's not meant for us. Don't worry if it feels disjointed or doesn't make sense. Just pass it on as it comes. It won't be wrong. When a person gives a spiritual message, whatever they say within that group must be done in truth. The trust and love that develops in a group cements relationships and builds a safe environment in which to receive other messages from spirit.

Meditation can provide us with a colour or a whole movie in black and white, each person's experience is unique to them. When our visions come through on a regular basis, we begin to want more or better clarity. But how do we obtain this? By simply asking our spiritual helpers. Sometimes it is easy to forgot that his is a two way process. We are not stumbling along unaided in the etheric veils. But sometimes it is possible to try too hard and miss what's blatantly obvious. Energy must flow freely so it can be processed by the minds. It cannot be forced. As we develop our psychic side, we must try and release any deep ingrained thoughts or beliefs that we have. If we don't, it could influence any messages that we might receive, or worse still, block things that we should have let through. Healing, whether it is spiritual or Angelic can help with this process.

Our ego is a force to be reckoned with too. It can get in the way of our spiritual progression and lead us on an entirely different pathway that is not nurturing. The deep need to progress and become a medium, could sometimes make us forget that we need a constant supply of spiritual growth to get there. We need to constantly ask for answers from our spiritual helpers and then listen for their response. If help is needed to get over a problem, ask for it. It may come direct from spirit or it may come via something/someone you're drawn to. Either way, once you we've made the request, help and answers will come to from many different sources.

I expect by the time this part of the book is reached, the reader might feel quite daunted. Don't be. We are all on a continual journey and it might take many lifetimes before we reach the end of it. But it is so worth the effort. Psychic Development requires us to be physically healthy. With spiritual awareness, comes awareness of the body. This doesn't mean we must all run to the gym and eat lettuce for the rest of our lives. Physical fitness can be obtained by holistic methods such as Crystal Therapy or Reiki. The mind and body must flow as one to be in balance with the physical and spiritual world.

When things go wrong

Alcohol and drugs are not very useful to the human body. Alcohol in moderation can be used for socialising, but that is all. I cannot stress enough that it should never be imbibed for at least 24hrs before serious meditation or immediately afterwards, this is because it alters the body's chemistry.

Any drug induced state of mind reflects an inaccurate image of ourselves and the situation we are in, which in turn damages any hope of spiritual growth. The purpose of meditation is to calm the mind and relax the body. Then self-healing can take place on a higher level. Cellular growth slows, wrinkles become fainter, because our metabolism is slowing down giving the body time to regenerate. Meditation relieves stresses and strains, stabilising blood pressure. All this will begin to happen within a few hours or days of commencing your meditation process.

When we receive sensory stimuli, we process it without control, even though we tell ourselves that we aren't. Our thoughts bounce around like a rubber ball, following our emotional and physical reactions. The first step in meditation is being able to gain control over the mind. It sounds easy! Believe me, it'll be the hardest thing a person will ever be asked to do. Mala beads can help. By concentrating on moving the beads through the fingers as we meditate, we're effectively telling the mind to concentrate on the task and nothing else. We now have control.

Another technique is to visualise a lit candle. Concentrate on the flame and if your attention begins to wane, pull it back to the flame. The mind has a way of leading us astray, for instance, let's say we have decided to meditate using a mantra. The word peace. In our mind we repeat it over and over again. Suddenly our mind adds war onto the end of peace. Now we think that war in such and such a place. Our mind flicks to a newspaper headline. We brought that paper in a shop and saw so and so. Now the mind has totally distracted us from the word peace and we're off on a rubber ball expedition with our thoughts.

What we need to do is acknowledge the distracting thought and then release it. This takes practise. Start of by meditating for five minutes a day and gradually build up to where you want to be. If we try to meditate for half an hour in the first instance, we will fail miserably and then think it's an impossible task. But if we start off with small steps, the confidence grows and the rubber ball effect will disappear.

A meditation to calm the mind and body

Take a moment to look at the picture of the woods. See the ancient trees, full of life and wisdom. The clearing looks peaceful, the grass green and bursting with energy. Take a breath and begin to calm your thoughts as you stare into the clearing.

Close your eyes and listen to your breath as you take a deep breath in through your nose and out through your mouth... in... out.. in... out...

Feel your body relaxing from your toes to your face.

I want you to visualise a gravel pathway winding ahead of you.

Feel its hard pebbles under your feet.

Directly in front of you is a dense forest, but it is not intimidating in anyway. On either side of you are tall trees, their branches sway gently above you in the morning breeze.

At their base are many flowers of all different colours and some colours that you don't recognise.

I want you to start walking down the path slowly.

Now you've come to a clearing and before you is a crystal clear waterfall.

The water is a deep sapphire blue.

Listen, as it cascades down the many rocks of a tall cliff into the rippling pool.

Go up the pool and dip your fingers in the blueness of the water, splash your face and feel its colour enfold you.

You are at peace, happy to just be in this magical place.

I want you to look around you.

Is anyone nearby?

Can you see any animals?

If there is a person, say hello.

Ask them for a name.

What are they wearing?

Sit beside the water. Listen for any sounds you might hear.

Feel warm, content and at peace with yourself.

How does the grass feel beneath you?

Now it's time to continue with your walk.

I want you stand up and if there is a person with you say goodbye.

Now I want you walk past the pool and feel yourself walking up a slight hill, it isn't hard, you're still walking slowly. The sky above you is a beautiful clear blue. Feel the colour energise you. Open yourself to it, feel it fill your body and cleanse your mind.

Once at the top of the hill take a deep breath, exhale. Feel the breeze take away your stresses and strains of the day. You can see for miles. The green of the grass, the many colours of the flowers, and the blue of the river as it meanders down the valley. See if there is somewhere you can sit.

There may be a bench, a rock or just the grass.

Pull the blue shawl, you feel around your shoulders together and quieten your mind. Nothing can harm you here. You are safe, relaxed. Relish in the warmth that floods your body.

Stay here a while. (You may stay for ten minutes to begin with and work your way up to more).

Now I'm afraid it's time to leave this place.

Stand up and walk back down the hill.

You go past the beautiful blue waterfall, through the forest and out of the other side.

The sky is still a beautiful blue and no clouds are in sight.

You are back on the gravel pathway and when you feel ready, open your eyes.

Self-Healing Meditation

Look at the picture. See the rainbow and its beautiful colours, arching across a sapphire sky. You can see for miles. Nothing is here to bother you. It's a safe, quiet place, where you can relax and just be.

Sit in a comfortable position, with your feet on the floor and your hands resting on your legs. Close your eyes and concentrate on just breathing in and out.

Visualise that a bright, white light is filling your feet.

As the light moves slowly up your body feel your muscles begin to relax.

Your mind is calm and everyday thoughts are beginning to still until all you can hear is the sound of your breath.

Now take your mind to any areas that hurt or are uncomfortable within your body.

See these areas surrounded by a dark shadow.

The light is still moving up your body and then it shines out from your eyes as if they've suddenly become a bright torch.

Now with your new torch like eyes, look at the areas on your body where the dark shadows are.

Feel that you are sending this healing light to the areas.

Watch as the dark areas begin to dissolve to be replaced with a small glow of white light.

Keep doing this until there are no more dark areas on your body.

Say these words now.

Healing light return to me my health and vitality

Say this as many times as you feel the need to.

When you feel the need to stop, see the light move away from your eyes, go back down your body, through your feet, and back into mother earth.

Then, when you are ready, open your arms feeling well and refreshed.

Using Mantic Tools

Mantic tools can be used by anyone who wishes to enhance their psychic skills. Some people use crystal balls, pendulums, coloured ribbons and various types of cards. These are all tools that help our spirit helpers to get a message across to us.

Choosing a mantic tool is very important. We need to feel comfortable with it. To find this type of comfortable vibration now is the time to use all our senses that we have been speaking about throughout this book.

Let us look at the pendulum. First of all we'll be attracted to a particular one, whether it be for its colour or shape. For a second, don't touch it, just look at it. Does it resonate with you? Is there a real urge to hold it? If so, the pendulum is psychically calling out to you. Our psyche will then acknowledge that call and translate it back to us via our senses.

Now pick it up. When held, does the hand it is in tingle? If it does, that means the pendulum is connecting with your energy. It recognises you as being compatible with it. If it felt heavy and cold in the hand, the crystal's not tuned into us and therefore needs to belong to someone else. Mantic tools allow us to focus on something, rather than letting our minds drift. It can be likened to a form of meditation. The tool will occupy the conscious mind allowing us to get on with receiving the spiritual information.

Trusting our intuition to guide us will bring the right mantic tool to our attention.

The Pendulum

The pendulum connects with our subconscious mind and our spirit helpers. It can be likened to a spiritual telephone. The pendulum, over time, will connect deeply with our vibration and will almost vibrate with energy as it connects with us. In other words, they become part of us because crystal has linked with our vibration as now resonates with us

When the pendulum has been chosen, before it's used, it is vital that it's cleansed. Crystals are like sponges. They suck in everyone's vibration that's handled them. None of these will help with Psychic Development.

Cleansing Methods

Under running water, with a small prayer.

Lay it on a crystal, Citrine bed for 24 hours.

Cover it in lavender for 24 hours.

Whatever way is comfortable for the owner should be used. The intuition will direct you.

No one should ask their pendulum personal questions. They are connected to the etheric realms and are an aid to help our spiritual growth, not our physical one. So yes or no spiritual questions should be asked, but sometimes they do work quite well when we need to find missing items.

Once cleansing has been achieved it is time to blend with the crystal. Meditation usually achieves the best result.

Pendulum Meditation

First, find a place where you will not be disturbed and then hold your pendulum in your non dominant hand. (If you're left handed, place in right and vice versa) Play some soothing music, sit down and close your eyes.

Visualise you are standing in the picture above. See and smell the beautiful, bluebell flowers. The trees are dappled with sunlight and the day is warm. In front of you is a narrow, dirt pathway, walk down it.

You pass the trees, breathing in the scent of the bluebells surrounding them, and then you come to a clearing. In the middle of a grassy meadow is your pendulum, standing upright as if it has just sprung from the ground.

It is very big and wide. You look tiny in comparison. Walk up to the crystal. It's quite secured, anchored to the ground by large roots.

If you look directly at it you will see a door appear. Go up to the door, turn the knob and open it.

Step inside. All around you is sparkling maze of crystal wands that match the colour of your pendulum. They criss cross in strange angles all around you and right in the centre of the crystal is a small stool and it's made from the same crystal as the pendulum. Go and sit down on it.

Look around you and see little pulses of lights within the crystal. They are like little rainbows hurrying from here to there. Watch them. Your body is relaxed and you feel at peace within the sanctuary of your pendulum.

Feel the walls of the pendulum move closer to you. You are not afraid because it feels like the pendulum is giving you a giant hug. Warmth radiates through you and you can feel the love from the crystal enfolding you. Take a deep breath and release it.

Say these words. *Heavenly father, divine spirit I ask that you send down your white light of energy to cleanse this crystal so that my energy can be aligned with it.*

Visualise your crystal room filling with a wonderful white light. It surrounds you, enters your body, until you, the crystal and the light are one single consciousness. Listen. Can you hear anything? A hum, a whisper, a fleeting noise. This is your crystal connecting to you.

Sit here awhile and enjoy this precious moment.

When you feel ready, visualise the white light receding until it is all gone. Open your eyes and you will be back in your chair, feeling energised and happy.

Know that you and your pendulum have become one and that your consciousness is aligned with that of the universe.

Using a Pendulum

Hold you pendulum with the crystal hanging over your index finger. Press the chain lightly in to your finger with your thumb. So that you're holding it lightly, yet not controlling its movements.

Say out loud or in your mind (as your pendulum is tuned into your thoughts now) which way for yes. Watch the pendulum to see which way it swings. Be patient. In the beginning the movements can be subtle. Once you've ascertained this, tell it to stop. Then say, which way for no. What movement for 'I'm not sure'.

Remember this is not a party trick to show off to friends. This is a deeply person attachment between you and the spirit realms. Have respect for it.

Cards

Many people use tarot or other cards to aid in their decision making, shed light on a future incident or enhance their spiritual readings. The card symbols and meanings resonate with the reader as if are stored in their psyche from birth.

Our spiritual helper/Guides can also use them and make themselves better understood to us. The fact that others can read the same cards for a person and give a different reading suggests they hold peoples vibrations and that's what us also picked up by the reader. The same reasoning can be applied to Runes or Flower readings. The object holds the persons vibration who first touched it and then the reader can focus on this to give a spiritual reading.

Developing your mantic tool link

Exercise One

Write down all the mantic tools you've heard about. Then, without referring to any books, write down as much as you can about what you know about them.

How you feel about them? Why do they resonate/don't resonate with you?

When you have done this you will have at least two tools that you feel drawn to.

You can then refer back to your notes, and how you felt, when you chose another at a later date.

Exercise Two

Now meditate on the tools you have felt drawn to. Your intuition will let you know which one, out of the two, will be good for you to use right now.

When you have decided on the tool, it is time to research all you can about it. Go on the internet, to a library, like-minded people and learn every single thing there is to know about this tool.

Once you have knowledge of how the tool functions, you can practise using it on a friend. Remember, your mantic tool works in conjunction with your intuition. So before you start any work with it, you need to say a protection prayer. As where there is light in the etheric realms, there is also darkness and you don't want to link up with that.

Pick a place that you will not be disturbed in. Light a white candle. Your mind should be calm and relaxed in order to understand the visions you might get through your mantic tool. Ask your guide to help you with the tool. With any spiritual work it is a union between two parties. Never try to work alone and bi-pass your spiritual helper.

Lastly, remember, the intuition is not about what we see, but about what we feel and sense too. Pay attention to what you feel as well as what you see.

When we get more confident with our spiritual connections we will realise that each person is an individual, their vibration is unique to them. What we sense and feel from that is for us to interpret in our own way.

Despite what is spread by scare mongers, your tool does not have the power to possess its owner. Universal Energy, that allows it to work, flows through *you.* Not the other way around. Now we have learnt to tune into energy from a person or object, it's time to use that knowledge to tune into our mantic tool, receive its energy and interpret the vision it sends us. This takes tireless practise. While we are doing this, our tool is aiding our psychic development. Readings will become more accurate, but do not get too complacent. Practise often and inform others that this is still a training phase. There is a world of 'bad psychics' out there, who give terrible advice, don't become one of them. Follow the spiritual laws and 'Do no harm' with your spiritual connections.

Here are some more exercises to develop your psychic ability

Exercise Three

Ask two friends, who know you are practising, if you may work on them. Fill in this guide

Persons name:

The mantic tool you chose to use:

Brief reading on what you got from the person using the tool: (Remember. This is not a test. Be calm, focus. If you get it wrong it doesn't matter at this stage. Practise makes perfect!)

How accurate where you? (Be honest as you are only fooling yourself.)

Was your subject pleased with what you gave them? Did you feel confident?

As we develop our inherent abilities we must remember that now we have a big responsibility towards the people we give messages too. It is a sad fact that tragedy, bad news and death are things we all have to deal with at some point in our lives. Grief is unfortunately an enemy we cannot hide from. As we become more proficient in our spiritual work, sometimes we will get visions of bad news when dealing with people.

If at any point a vision of death or a tragedy is received how do we relay this back to someone who has come to you for upliftment?

Before you answer, meditate on this question. What does your higher intuition tell you to do?

Here is an example of a scenario

A person who comes to you for spiritual advice is having an affair with a married man who tells her he will leave his wife for her. Your mantic tool and intuition tells you this will never happen. What do you say? A bad psychic might say... you're being used. He'll never leave his wife. You're being a naive fool. All of which will cause the lady great distress.

A good psychic will say...your friend does care for you, but let's look at the situation rationally. You could tell them, he has his own house, good job, pretty wife and young children. Why do you think he will give it all up? Are you sure he will?

Let the person form the conclusion. You have given them the bigger picture; maybe put something in the open she is unwilling to face herself, without causing distress. Sometimes you might become a mini counsellor at times. Try not to give advice, even if they say 'what do you think I should do?'

It is not our place to tread the pathway of others. We must allow them to take their own journeys, make their own mistakes. If we can ease their burdens for a bit, then we have done what we are supposed to do.

Spiritual Beings

Now our intuition is awake, this is a good time to meet and understand the people in spirit who are helping us with our spiritual growth. There are many that look after us; some will always remain nameless as that is what they prefer. It doesn't mean they don't want you to know it, it seems that when you leave this physical life the 'name tag' we had when alive becomes irrelevant. To explore the different spiritual helpers we need to understand their function and how they can help us.

Master Guides

We have one "Master Guide". This spirit person knows us better than we do because they have been by our side throughout every life we have ever lived. This guide will never leave us until we have learnt all the lessons that we need to.

Although they help us on a daily basis, they aren't with us twenty-four hours a day. We can still live our lives without fear that we're constantly being watched by spiritual eyes.

Spirit Guides

These spirit people have experienced life on the earth many, many times. Instead of returning to the one consciousness, they have decided to stay on the etheric planes and help others in the physical world, with spiritual development. They can be souls of people that we've known in past lives. Maybe this would explain why we instinctively know that we can trust them. These wise people have made arrangements with us before we're born: to guide us and help us learn the lessons we line up for ourselves. Also, to gently remind us when we're a bit 'off our pathway' from our original plan for this lifetime.

Because they have no corporeal substance, guides can manifest into any form that is acceptable to us. Human form, animal, a crystal, colours etc. Many people have Native American spiritual helpers. This is because they were/are such a spiritual race of people they feel the need to come back and help, even though in the physical world their culture and way of life has been grossly misinterpreted and misunderstood.

These guides can lead you to your animal totem, animal guide or power animal, which are said to be the essence of an animal that has passed to the spirit realms. Anyone can benefit from accessing his or her totem animal. According to some Native American beliefs, we have two animal guides who walk with us - one on our left and one on our right. These animals appear to us in dreams and visions to guide and protect us along the path of life.

Whatever guide we have, they arrive with their own personalities, and their own ways of communicating. They will stay with us even if we choose to ignore them, and they will continue to love and honour us throughout our life. One of the misconceptions about a spirit guide is that they are here to serve us. This isn't correct. It's a partnership with no seniority as the spirit world operates on the same 'free will' parameters as the physical.

Guides provide guidance and insight into situations. We can either choose to ignore their advice or use it. They can stay with us for long periods of time, or a very brief period, depending on what we need to learn. Some people never get to 'see' their guide as they often decide it isn't important that we dwell on what they look like. We are spirit encased in a vehicle for mobility. Once this is of no use, what it looked like becomes irrelevant. They've no need to manifest into this vehicle again when they are so much more than that. So they often appear as energy, swirls of colour or an outline within a nebulous mist.

Spiritual Helpers

Helpers are like guides, but often they are interested in some facet of our life. For example, if you're a carpenter, a helper who was once in that trade may take an interest in what you're doing and guide you to make something astonishing. Like attracts like in the world of spirit, so whatever we have a talent for here, you can be assured there's a spirit person with the same talent helping you.

Doorkeeper

If we channel, (trance work) then a helper in spirit is often appointed to help us. They'll protect our physical body and guard against anything happening that we don't feel comfortable with. These highly evolved beings of light will sometime show themselves to those people who have the gift of clairvoyance.

Angels

Contrary to belief, angels are not our Aunties, Uncles, Mothers or Fathers. These etheric beings have never lived on the third dimensional plane (linear) and they've no free will because they obey the will of god. Angels function on a higher vibration and dimension than spirit guides. Angels protect, inspire and empower us; guides offer direct advice or instruction.

There are three spheres of angels, the third one being closest to God. While they are an excellent conveyor of universal love, they're not always equipped to deal with earthy problems. The third and second spheres have no understanding of human emotions and rely on the angels on the first sphere to interpret them.

We have two angels constantly by our side. But they will never intervene on our behalf unless we ask them too. Guardian angels are those who have been by our side for every life time we have ever experienced. They can be felt like old friends. We also have an angel for each lifetime who works with the guardian angel.

Once you let these wonderful beings into your life nothing is impossible any more.

Spiritual Abilities

Not everyone works with spirit people in the same way. We all have different ways of communicating with them, just as we have different ways of communicating with the living.

Here are a few exercises that you can use to communicate.

Exercise One
For Clairaudience

You may wonder how you can tell if the voices you hear are psychic information or your own daily thoughts. This is how to distinguish the two. Intuition will speak in a kind, loving, positive way, the 'self' talk tends to be harsher and more critical.

Sit down and breathe deeply. Ask your guides for protection and imagine a shield of golden light is around your ears.

Now visualise that an old - fashioned radio dial is in front of you. With this dial you can tune your frequency of hearing to a new one.

Gently turn the dial, and as you do, sense a subtle sound change within as you adjust the frequency. Listen. What can you hear? Is it a distant voice, a song, a crackle of energy, whatever it is, keep turning the dial until it becomes clearer.

Stay here for a while and listen.

When you're ready, move the dial back to the start position. Breathe in deeply and as you exhale, open your eyes.

It is a good idea to note whatever information you might receive. At first you may hear nothing, but keep on doing the exercise. After a while your ears will tune in automatically whenever you focus and open up your spiritual ear chakra centres.

Exercise Two

For Clairsentience

Those people, who are emotional and sensitive to others, will be able to feel other people's moods too. When this gift is fully developed it is possible to progress and feel the moods of spirit people who have died with unresolved issues?

Sit down, breathe deeply, and ask your guide for protection.

Now imagine you're a fish in the ocean. Enjoy the feeling of freedom as you glide through the beautiful, crystal clear, blue water.

Now imagine you're part of a brightly coloured school of fish. You swim in rhythm with your group, sense its mood and shift your direction in perfect time and rhythm with the others.

Now imagine yourself to be able to feel the mood of the whole oceanic world. You can automatically sense and locate where to feed, play swim and feel safe. You are in total harmony with the ocean world.

Stay here a while and play.

When you are ready, take a deep breath in, exhale and open your eyes.

Again, this takes practice to get right. Just keep doing it until you feel that connection.

Exercise Three

For Clairvoyance

Take a deep breath and ask your guide for protection. I want you to visualise a protective bubble of light around yourself. Allow your eyes to go out of focus and concentrate on your third eye, that's situated just in - between your eyebrows.

Close your eyes lightly and focus your mind on the images that you see behind your eyelids. What do you see?

Are their lights?

Flashes of colour?

Can you see a small square screen with people moving very quickly or is it just random shapes?

Don't do this for too long as you'll begin to tire.

Practise this often and you'll get surprising results.

Protection

We love guides because of the energy they project onto us when we connect with them. But before an attempt to speak to anyone on a spirit is made, we need to protect ourselves. With every yin there is a yang and the opposite to light is dark. The brighter the light on the spirit plains, the darker the light that we'll attract into our energy from the lower astral planes. Always visualise a white light around the physical body and say a small prayer of protection. Ask your guides for their help in keeping you safe.

The only way I can explain the dark energy that lurks on the periphery of the light, is by breaking it down into separate parts.

1. Every dark thought a person has creates an energy that goes out into the cosmos. This thought energy then bounces around until it finds someone to accept it.

2. Those who have led a murderous life on earth wander around, unable to find the light, looking for a person on the earth to influence so they can find life again.

3. Inhuman shapes that, I can only describe as a cold energy residue, which can attach themselves to our auras and feed off our energy.

The spirit world is not all harps and roses, some aspects of it must never be tapped into. The relationship with our guide is based on trust, because trust brings with it the highest possible energy. As previously mentioned in this book, because of the nature of spiritual growth, some guides will move on after a period of time. Having spent a long time developing our communication with them, this can be upsetting. We are physical and therefore have strong emotional attachments. But we need to stay positive; because change means that we are growing and moving forward spiritually.

When a new guide is introduced, it is done slowly, so that feelings can adjust on both levels and the new energy can be explored. Guides are very aware that this sudden change can knock our confidence and cause us to make irrational choices in our spiritual development. Sometimes the old guide will stay for a time, offering reassurance and help in the transition. Either way, the change will be as smooth as possible.

Dreams play a large part in our relationships with guides. They provide a theatre where we can act out scenes when our conscious mind has gone to sleep. Guides work with us in a structured way that we can understand easily. They'll use language/symbols pulled from our minds that we will instantly recognise. Asking the right question is very important. Keep it simple at first.

We are human, so names are important to us. It's a form of communication that we learn from a child. A lot of people feel passionate about labelling their guides with a name. Otherwise they feel they don't have that personal connection with them. When a name is asked for and it's not forthcoming, don't force the issue. Remember, it's the signature of the guide's energy which is more important, not a label. That is similar to a name, because when it comes again, it's instantly recognisable.

Images of guides are similar to names. The image they give to us depends on what we will best respond to. For those who teach spiritual matters, their guides might work within a team so therefore they have no specific name to offer. Just be assured that they have many facets and therefore can offer a huge amount of knowledge to the teacher.

As we progress on our spiritual paths we are bound to come up against obstacles. If for whatever reason a person feels they've done something wrong in their spiritual work, there's no need to feel that it's the end of the world. The very fact that the person has thought about the wrong doing will summon spiritual intervention. Help and guidance is always given on a positive level and no experience we go through is ever wasted. Without total belief and trust in our guides and helpers any spiritual work will be impeded. Belief feeds the power and intensity of our guide, which in turn gives us that deep personal connection to them.

But it's not all work and no play with your spiritual helpers. Guides have a sense of humour too; don't be afraid to laugh with them. Laughter makes us feel good, which in turn raises our vibration, keeping channels open and cements relationships within the spirit and physical world.

Contacting Spirit Guides

There are many ways to contact Spirit Guides! One way is through meditation. Guided Meditations, aimed specifically at meeting a guide, are extremely helpful. If we're too busy living and don't remember to meditate and listen, our dreams then become the only time our chattering mind can quieten enough to receive a spiritual message. There are many forms of communication.

Automatic Writing

Automatic writing is a way of receiving direct communication from guides and helpers. When it's combined with meditation, the mind is freed from its limitations and allows incoming messages to be received. The physical hand will begin to write in script that isn't theirs. The messages are usually very insightful, full of love, wisdom and guidance.

Synchronicity

This is an indication that we have a Spirit Guide or an angel trying to get our attention. They will place, books, articles, TV programs or people in our path that will contain a message in some form. The contact is very gentle at first, until we become more familiar with their unique vibration. One of humanities greatest blocks, is the unrealistic expectation at what receiving guidance should be like. If a booming voice or an apparition is expected, then prepared to be very disappointed. Contact comes on a deep, intuitive level. It's a feeling of 'knowing'. The art of perceiving our guides comes from the ability to comfortably tune in and listen to these subtleties and accept them.

How do we know when a guide is near us?

The physical world is based on the five sensory perceptions we as humans use. Those in spirit use our sixth sense, hence why we need to develop it. Guides make subtle suggestions through our sixth sense. The more we speak to them the more they'll respond.

There are many ways that Spirit Guides will alert you to their presence. Many use scents to signal they are there. We'll get a whiff of some fragrance that has no "physical source" or explanation. Other times the fragrance will have specific memories for us. Sound is another way. Some guides will use auditory signals such as "chimes" that only the individual it's meant for will hear. There are many other ways including chills, cold chills or goose bumps. Spirit energy definitely, at times, seems to move in mysterious ways.

While most of the time, we are in the 'light' when we speak to our guides, under some circumstances, such as Automatic Writing or channelling, the darkness will try an make an appearance. But if basic precautions are adhered to, prayer spoken with intent and lighting a white candle, we are protected from any encounters with negative beings.

Here is a good prayer to use:

Heavenly father, divine spirit. I ask for a ring of protection to be placed around me, this house and all who dwell under its roof whether they are an animal or human. I ask for just my guides and helpers to come and work with me in love and light. Amen.

This is the time to also remember that we NEVER work alone when it comes to the spirit world. Always ask your Guides for help with your spiritual and physical pathway. This is one of the subtle ways in which Angels and Spirit Guides differ from each other. Angels, especially Guardian Angels, will rarely intervene unless asked. Spirit Guides however, will help up to a point without being asked, but they are also bound by certain spiritual laws from interfering with our lives.

I've mentioned before about 'free will'. It really means that we can do whatever we want to even if it means ignoring the lessons we originally set up for ourselves. In this instance our guides and angels cannot interfere with our choice, however unwise it may be. They will help as much as they can, but they will not live our life for us.

Seeing our Spirit Guides depends very much on the individual. Guides exist on a non-physical, vibrational plane. It takes a tremendous amount of effort for them to adjust their frequency so that we can see them. As they adjust their vibration, we at the same time must raise ours. It is always a two way connection here.

A good way to connect is to sit down, close your eyes and imagine there is a white screen in front of you. Ask your guide to appear on it. At first you must just get a shadowy outline, a vague face shape - persevere. Rome wasn't built in a day. If you don't see a guide, start creating an image on the screen. A garden. Add chairs, flowers and lake, and then be observant. Someone/thing may appear that you didn't put there.

Meet your guide Meditation

Step One

Find a quiet place to meditate. Today you're going to ask only non-personal Yes or No questions to your guide. Outside is excellent. Especially if you can lean up against a big, old tree.

Relax your body and mind. Close your eyes.

Take three slow deep breaths and relax. Open your mind to 'listen'.

Begin by sending a thought to your guide....Hello! Are you ready to talk to me?

Now relax and allow the answer to come into your thoughts - not in physical words - but in a thought. You should hear an affirmative answer. YES!

Now ask a question, such as.....Is it sunny today? You should hear the correct answer.

Is today Sunday? Again - You should hear the correct answer.

Continue with more non-personal questions that can be answered with Yes or No.

Don't be concerned if you don't hear anything straight away. This needs to be practised. You're altering your brain waves to hear the messages. If you're not certain that the messages are not your own thoughts - time and practice will allow you to feel the difference.

As you get to know your guide – you'll talk to them more easily.

Step Two

You're going to ask non-personal questions again.

Think... Hello. You should sense a greeting.

Now ask... Are you here to answer my questions? Wait for the reply.

Begin with a series of simple questions which will enable you to practice listening.

At this stage it is acceptable to ask for a name should you wish one.

If you have trouble understanding the name - listen hard - then come as close to what you can hear as possible.

When a name is agreed upon - your higher self will sense that it's the right one. This is called a frequency signature.

Now call the guide by name and then ...May I ask you some Yes and No questions?

Wait for an answer. It should be immediate.

Relax - listen - and be patient. It's very important that you don't get frustrated as this will lower your vibration. Remember you need to raise yours to meet theirs.

Ask questions about your spirit guide and their place in your life. It's best, at first, to only talk to one guide. This will then help you get used to their frequency.

It's very important that you establish a comfortable relationship with your main guide first. Yes and No questions about them first.

Did you ever live on the physical Earth plane?

Did we know each other?

Were we related?

The more time you take to communicate with them, the greater the connection you'll have with them.

Remember, the connection with your guides and spiritual helpers is a deeply personal thing. You cannot be guided by other people's experiences. Once you've made this connection you will truly have a friend for life who you can trust with all you're thought's, good and bad.

Evolving Spiritually through Psychic Development

By now everyone who has read this far through the book should be aware of their spiritual connection and have a good understanding of the mechanics of it. Now we need to talk about spirituality. The deepest part within that gives us the drive to know more about the spirit world and ourselves and to read this book.

Our spiritual self is higher than our conscious awareness, and as we evolve as spiritual beings we are guided by Ascended Masters, Spirit guides and Angels. These transient beings serve the 'one consciousness'. Some people say this is god, but spirituality can mean different things to different people. To me it's an expression of whatever is positive. It places us on a path of universal understanding. It's a positive vibration that brings comfort to those who live in this sometimes troubled world.

We hold within us three separate worlds. The body, soul and spirit. Our physical body houses our emotions and thoughts, defining who we are, yet it also limits us. We can be so much more if only we strive to find the knowledge that will empower us and make us grow. Unfortunately, along the path of evolvement, we've lost our connection to the infinite. If we cannot connect to our spirit, we can't connect with the soul.

As spiritual beings we've become dysfunctional and forever yearning for something that will make our life better, easier or richer. We throw our hands up in frustration and say 'if there is a god, why does he let me go through this?' Yet at the same time we fight wars to gain 'free will' and be able to live our lives without interference. We were given free will to learn from mistakes and disappointments, not to blame others for them.

The body is like a diamond with many facets. Sadly, many of us have forgotten how to explore them. Yet it's all there to be tapped into and the life you want will begin to open up to you and change. You will find a purpose and those around you will benefit from it as well. Just as you throw a pebble into a lake, the ripples it produces are your thoughts and words touching others.

The Etheric body

Jesus said in John 6:63:

"It is the Spirit who gives life; the flesh profits nothing;"

That small statement reiterates the fact that it's the etheric/spirit body which gives us the vitality, health, life and organisation to the physical body. The Etheric body has seven major energy centres called chakras which run vertically down the centre of the body and hundreds of smaller ones that are spread out all over the body. It's composed of two auric layers. One extends almost a foot from the physical body and the other about three feet. In this modern world we take what the physical body looks like as a defining factor of who we are. This is a very narrow view of a wider landscape.

The Spirit incarnates into the physical body for the purpose of experiencing growth. Life is an endless school of learning. What we fail to grasp in one life, we will learn in another. The spirit needs to play different roles in order to grow and learn, but ultimately it will reintegrate into the whole. Hence the term used that when we die we go 'home'.

When we surrender the earthly vehicle that is known as the 'body', our spirit is the only part of the human experience that leaves. It takes with it all the memories from the life we've just lived as well as our past life experiences. This is our spiritual growth and development evolving.

But we must also understand that different religions have their own viewpoints on life and death. There is no monopoly on truth, so we cannot force beliefs onto others. Everyone should follow the path that suits them, but I do believe their destination will always remain the same.

Physical Body

The physical body is composed off solids, liquids, and gases, but it depends upon the Etheric Body for its good health. Our body is just an embellished carriage for the spirit. It's governed by our feelings, thoughts, and subconscious reactions. The reason we need the body is to allow us to interact with the world.

The soul stands between the two and yet it is part of them both. It is linked to the one consciousness through the spirit and to the physical world through the body. Although the spirit cannot act directly upon the body, it can influence it. The dependence of spirit on the physical body is like the dependence of a ship in a dry-dock. Once the ship leaves the dry dock they become free floating. The body can be thought of as the spirit's dry-dock, and death just allows it to float free from its earthly restrictions.

Astral Body

The astral body is aligned with the physical body and is of a lower vibration when it's attached to us. The astral body can transcend time and space and when the time comes for it to detach –death- there is a feeling of separation, such as a rushing or being pulled along at a great speed. When in the astral planes of spiritual existence, the remains of our physical filter falls away and we are able to see, hear and feel everything in a blink of an eye.

The Soul

There's often confusion between the words Spirit and Soul. Some say it's the same energy, just with a different name. Ancient Greeks called it our 'perfect nature.' But there's a huge difference between the two. Spirit is that part of us which enables us to commune with God. It's known as the element of God-consciousness. Self dwells in the soul; it defines who we really are. Some people say when they look into eyes, they can see the person's soul. That could be true. They could be seeing the true image of that person and not just the physical body that houses it.

The soul is our birth right and is represented as feminine. It expresses our moral values through ideals, Conscience, and Intuition. It also possesses 'Free Will'. It stands between the spirit and the body, binding the two together. Every living thing, whether it is an animal or a human being, has a soul. It's that part of us which is immortal, often existing for hundreds of years and it's where the consciousness and virtues cultivated in each lifetime are left.

Because the soul is the central point of consciousness it includes the Physical, Etheric, Astral, and Mental consciousness. If it were seen, it would appear as a white and golden light with sparkling energy within it. Some areas can appear dark; but this just means there are areas which are waiting to be unfolded, but not necessarily within the life that the person is living now.

A person creates their life experiences by the choices they make before they are born. Being eternal, the consequences of our actions will always come back to us, because we have to live with them forever. It is the law of infinity.

Karma or the spiritual law of cause and effect is our own process of being responsible for what we create. This spiritual principle is found in many other religions as well. Throughout life, our karma is designed so that each trial it goes through will not be too great for us to endure. It is ever changing. Growing and learning, using free will to explore, create and discover.

Reading and exploring this book is the kick start that you need to cultivate your spiritual development and from here you will go onto explore many more avenues that will open up to you. From now on the world will seem a much larger place, full of knowledge and experience's just waiting for you to explore it.

www.ingramcontent.com/pod-product-compliance
Lightning Source LLC
Chambersburg PA
CBHW040054160426
43192CB00002B/63